God's
Secret
Agent

THE SERVANT'S CRY

The man of God went out to serve,
Never seeking a reward;
He only saw the need of those
Endeavoring to teach the Word.

Houses divided — without unity —
Shepherds and flocks with no plan or goal;
Multitudes waiting to be reached,
The man of God wept tears from his soul.

So many directions — so few to assist,
Spirits are willing but flesh is untrained;
"I'm only one man!" the servant cried out,
"How shall I finish this task that I've claimed?"

God saw the heart of His servant so true,
And He said, "My son, you've done well;
It's you I've anointed to teach and to train,
Just go where I lead and my Kingdom will swell."

"As a great sea My people will cover the land,
As they're taught and are willing to learn.
And as each does his best and there's no more to do,
Christ Jesus, My Son, will return."

Ginny
November 14, 1986
For Ron.

GOD'S SECRET AGENT

By
Ron Kite

RON KITE MINISTRIES
P. O. Box 33110
Tulsa, OK 74153

ISBN 0-942847-01-6

FOREWORD

Dedication

It is with a warm heart and a very special thanks that I dedicate this book to a very beloved friend, comrade, and pastor without equal . . .

One of the greatest privileges of my life has been sitting under the teaching ministry of Billy Joe Daugherty and working on the staff of the great Victory Christian Center of Tulsa, Oklahoma.

The spirit of a true pastor's heart is transferred to many. There is no way a member, or even a non-member, can sit under this great man of God and not hear his cry. The cry is the message of Ephesians Chapter 4 — that in order for God to fulfill His plan in the earth, BELIEVERS must get involved and begin doing the work of the ministry.

That is the message of this book.

The challenge of this message has a built-in reward. For, as thousands of enthusiastic able ministers — individuals from all walks of life — have learned at Victory, when you catch the pastor's vision, and when you endeavor to help the man of God fulfill the dream God has given him . . . then your own dreams are fulfilled. It is in planting the seeds of Love, Finances, Hard Work, that you are able to reap fulfillment and purpose in your own life.

I want to thank Billy Joe Daugherty for sharing that message — God's message — over and over and over for the last nine years. It has become a part of us, a way of life, and a message we now are compelled within ourselves to share with others.

We believe this book will help you to reach your dreams.

Ron Kite

TABLE OF CONTENTS

Foreword (Dedication) 7

Preface 11

1   LIFELINE BEHIND THE SCENES. 15

    To Be Like Him

2   FAITHFULNESS BRINGS INCREASE 23

    Being Available
    Being Faithful

3   THE NOBLEST CALLING. 31

    How We Perish
    An Early Grave
    Their Place — My Place
    Breaking Free

4   THE DUPLICATION PRINCIPLE. 39

    God's Plan for Your Talents

5   YOU ARE PART OF GOD'S PLAN 47

    Who Are the Saints?
    What Is the Work of the Ministry?
    Why Isn't Everyone Involved?
    A Miracle Is Squelched
    Your Part

6   YOU ARE AN EXTENSION OF THE ARMS
    OF JESUS 55

    Understanding the Ministry of Helps
    Disciples in the Helps Ministry
    God's Agents in Action
    Your Assignment

7   GOALS FOR GROWTH.....................69

8   REWARDS OF SERVING...................85

Expect A Reward
Examine Your Motives
Heavenly Rewards
Earthly Rewards
The Ultimate Reward

9   YOU ARE GOD'S AGENT 99

Don't Miss the Boat
Put God to the Test
Make a Commitment Today

COMMITMENT CARD

PREFACE

In the ministry assigned by God to the Believers, there is a place for every person. There are specialized areas of talent in each life. There is a place where YOU fit into the Body, and no one else can fill that place just the way you can.

Your job is to find out what God wants you to do and then to be faithful and consistent in doing what God has assigned to you.

The purpose of this book is to help encourage:

❏ Those who have experienced a poor self-image and felt there was nothing they were qualified to do.

❏ Those who have developed gifts and talents in the secular world, yet have felt there was nothing they had to offer that the Church could use.

❏ Believers with gifts and talents who, when they endeavored to get involved, were told they could not help.

❏ Many who now are discouraged because they have been told that they were not "ministers" and therefore could not pray for or be of help to the lost, the sick, or the hurting masses.

❏ Those who have never realized or been taught the true meaning of the word "Servanthood."

This message is intended to motivate the believer whose heart is desirous to work — as a secret agent for God — but who has never been recognized or encouraged to get involved.

This book is also written as an encouragement for the pastors who are stretching themselves beyond human limitations and who are desperately hoping to see the light at the end of the tunnel.

God HAS that light ahead for you.

And he gave some, apostles; and some prophets; and some, evangelists; and some, pastors and teachers;

FOR THE PERFECTING OF THE SAINTS FOR THE WORK OF THE MINISTRY, for the edifying of the body of Christ:

Till we ALL come in the unity of the faith, and of the knowledge of the Son of God, unto the measure of the stature of the fulness of Christ . . .

From whom the whole body fitly joined together and compacted BY THAT WHICH EVERY JOINT SUPPLIETH.

Ephesians 4:11-13, 16

CHAPTER 1

Lifeline Behind the Scenes

Several years ago, my wife and I were able to take some time off from our busy schedule in the ministry to not only be with each other, but to get alone with God and to make sure we were doing what He had told us.

It is important for everyone to stop now and then and make sure we are on target. Often, we get so involved in the work of the ministry and what God originally told us to do that we forget to listen to see if there are any new instructions.

Someone once said, "We get so involved in the forest that we don't see the trees." Sometimes we need to step out of the forest and take a look at the trees and smell the flowers.

My wife, Ginny, and I saw this opening in our schedule and we were blessed with a very spacious room on a small island in the Caribbean.

Our room was in the shape of a triangle, and two of the walls were of glass, overlooking the beautiful deep clear blue water of the Caribbean.

The hotel sat on the end of the six mile island — an area still uninhabited and almost isolated from people. It is one of the few places I have seen still unspoiled by people. There were no televisions in the rooms, nor telephones — which is a blessing in itself.

The inhabited part of the island, the native population, had 100,000 people living within one square mile area. Their source of income was from tourists who would visit the island shops in a small eight to ten block strip.

There were very few private cars on the island. Most of the natives walked or rode bikes.

The most prestigious job was that of the taxicab drivers, who would spend years working for someone else and dream of the day they could own their own cab.

Walking along the almost deserted beach was a delight. The water was so crystal clear that you could see the shells on the bottom, as well as fish and other sea life. It seemed as though you could reach your hand out and touch a fish or pick up a shell, but they were actually many feet away.

The beaches were the cleanest and nicest kept of any we have seen anywhere in the world.

One morning as my wife was gazing out of our glass-walled room, she asked me, "Ron, why are the beaches so nice here?"

What she was saying was: "Here we are on an almost unknown island in the Caribbean and inhabited by a people with the most elementary civilization . . . And we live in the U.S.A. with all of America's engineering and technology . . . Yet, our beaches are dirty, smelly, and for the most part are no comparison with the beaches directly in front of our hotel."

As I thought about the question my wife had posed to me, and in seeking God in prayer about other things, He showed me some miraculous revelations in His Word concerning His servants — and especially about those who work behind the scenes.

The next morning I arose early as usual to seek the Lord and enjoy quiet fellowship with Him. As I gazed out the window at 5:00 a.m. to catch the first rays of the early morning light, I noticed that on the beach, directly in front of our hotel, were twelve men.

As I watched them, I realized that each one had approximately twenty-five feet of beach that he was individually responsible for.

These men, or perhaps we should say natives of the island, were picking up all of the debris that had washed up during the night. They were picking up seaweed, driftwood, dead fish, large shells, coconuts, bottles and other things.

They used large containers similar to five-gallon paint buckets to haul the junk they picked up. Then they placed the full containers on their heads and carried them approximately one mile around the bend of the island to a dumping ground where the wind would carry the odor of the dead fish out to sea.

The natives would make several trips and continue picking up the large objects and dumping their loads around the bend until the beach looked good.

But then . . . they began to use their fingers as rakes. Bending over, they would scratch their entire section, digging into the sand and picking up all small shells and foreign objects that were buried just below the surface.

They would once again put this debris into their large containers and continue taking them to the dumping ground until the entire beach was raked spotless by their fingers.

Lastly, they would take a large leaf of some variety of palm and sweep each section they were responsible for . . . until the area about them looked absolutely beautiful — perfect — and natural — as if it always stayed that way.

Now, these men worked from around 4:30 a.m. until 7:30 every morning. While we were there (for a week and a half), there were three storms. And even on the mornings it was raining, the men were out there picking up the debris which the storms had brought in during the night.

As I arose early that morning after my wife had questioned me, the Lord showed me that THESE TWELVE NATIVES WHO WERE CLEANING

THE BEACH EACH MORNING ARE SIMILAR TO, OR COMPARABLE TO, THOSE FAITHFUL MEN AND WOMEN WHO ARE WORKING IN AREAS BEHIND THE SCENES IN MINISTRIES ALL ACROSS THIS COUNTRY.

These men were faithfully cleaning the beach each morning — unnoticed. I would say that 95 percent of the people on the island never knew they were there.

Why?

Well, for one reason, they had finished their job and were gone before most people ever got out of bed.

So I'm convinced that most of the tourists think the beach is naturally clean and have no earthly idea that anyone was ever there.

I also believe that the people who lived on the populated portion of the island never knew they were there, for they were concerned with the items they were selling and with the taxicab business.

But I am also convinced that if these men DID NOT clean the beach each day that in a few months, not only would the tourists notice, but also those who lived on the island.

For once the beaches became covered with seaweed, driftwood, trash and dead fish . . . and became dirty and smelly . . . the tourist agencies would direct the tourists to a different island.

19

Without the tourists, the hotels wouldn't have any business. And without finances, the hotels would begin to depreciate.

The taxicab drivers, who depend upon tourists, would eventually no longer have the elite jobs, because there would be no one for them to haul around.

The shops would no longer prosper, or even exist, because the taxis would have no people to bring to them.

And, eventually, the island would no longer be a vacation hideaway. All because the natives — that 95 percent of the people on the island never knew existed — stopped cleaning the beaches.

To Be Like Him

Unfortunately, this is a true comparison of many godly men and women today who are called to serve our Lord Jesus Christ in the area of helping behind the scenes.

The Bible says we are to be as Jesus. If we believe Jesus is our example, and if we are to be LIKE HIM, we must be servants. Jesus said in Mark 10:45, *"The Son of man came not to be ministered unto, but to minister..."* That is to say, "I came not to BE SERVED, but TO SERVE."

He further instructed His disciples that if they had any desire to be great — noticed — important — they must be the "SERVANT OF ALL."

Second Corinthians 12:28 says that God placed each member in the body JUST AS HE PLEASED OR DESIRED.

You see, He has given each of us a gift, a talent, a skill, or an ability — so we as members can come together and USE our God-given talents WITH ALL OUR HEART SERVING HIS KINGDOM.

Why then are the great majority of lay people not operating in their God-given gifts and talents? Many do not even know that they have any gifts or talents. If they do know, they do not seem to know how or where to get plugged in. And the sad part about it is, the church leadership as a whole has never recognized that servants (those who work behind the scenes) are just as much in the ministry as the apostle, prophet, evangelist, pastor or teacher.

But . . . without the servants:

❏ The church will not grow.

❏ Signs and wonders will not follow.

❏ The masses will not be reached.

CHAPTER 2

Faithfulness Brings Increase

What we have just shared may be new to some of you. So, before we go any farther, let's read...

ACTS 6:1-4,7,8

> *And in those days, when the number of the disciples was multiplied, there arose a murmuring of the Grecians against the Hebrews, because their widows were neglected in the daily ministration.*
> *Then the twelve called the multitude of the disciples unto them, and said, it is not reason that we should leave the word of God, and serve tables.*
> *Wherefore, brethren, look ye out among you seven men of **honest report, full of the Holy Ghost** and **wisdom**, whom we may appoint over this business.*
> *But we will give ourselves continually to prayer, and to the ministry of the word.*
> *And the **word of God increased;** and **the number of the disciples multiplied** in Jerusalem greatly; and a great company of the priests were obedient*

> *to the faith.*
> *And Stephen, **full of faith and power,***
> *did **great wonders and miracles***
> *among the people.*

Here we have a beautiful example of the disciples selecting seven men to assist them in overseeing the ministry of distributing food and clothing to the widows.

Now, the ministry duties the twelve had been involved with (caring for the widows) were necessary. They were of God. But these duties were taking a great deal of their time — time they needed to use for praying, seeking and doing God's further assignments.

The twelve never said that they would neglect the widows, nor did they feel these duties were no longer important. The daily ministration to the needy was not only to continue, but continue with someone in charge who was full of the Holy Ghost and full of wisdom (both practical and godly).

The author of Acts relates (v. 3) that the men chosen were to be *"of honest report, **full of the Holy Ghost and wisdom."*** These men were to be well tested and proven. They were to be men of integrity . . . men having a good reputation . . . men known to be faithful in areas in which they were involved.

Such men were selected. And the Bible says that the daily ministry to the widows was not neglected, the poor were cared for as directed by God; yet, the disciples — who had received instructions to preach and teach — were freed up and were enabled to spend their time in the Word and prayer.

The result was that, each time the twelve came before the people, they had taken the time to PRAY AND SEEK GOD. The GLORY of God was upon them. They spoke with such WISDOM that the people marvelled. The Word went forth with GREAT POWER. And because the crowds were receiving "hot (spiritual Word) banquets," SIGNS AND WONDERS followed.

There was a GREAT REVIVAL! The church EXPLODED!

But — I want you to note that this happened because of those seven men who were selected to take over the "mundane" duties of "waiting on tables." Because of their obedience to SERVE, those who were called and anointed to preach and teach (in this case, the disciples) were ABLE to carry out what God had told them to do.

In other words, because of helpers behind the scenes, taking the load off the disciples, the disciples were released to pray and spend time in the Word . . . with the results:

❏ THE WORD OF GOD INCREASED.

❏ THE DISCIPLES MULTIPLIED (THE CHURCH GREW IN NUMBER).

❏ GREAT WONDERS AND MIRACLES OCCURRED AMONG THE PEOPLE.

❏ A GREAT COMPANY OF THE PRIESTS WERE OBEDIENT TO THE FAITH.

God's "Secret Agents" — faithful servants working in the background — resulted in mighty manifestations of the glory and power of God — through those who had been called to the forefront.

Being Available

It is interesting to note that the disciples who are now (in Acts 6) preaching and working miracles actually began by helping Jesus. They had started out in the background...just being available to aid and assist Him in whatever He needed done at the time.

They were the ones who had spent 3½ years with Jesus,

❑ sitting at His feet

❑ hearing God's Word

❑ helping Jesus whenever they could by:

- preparing the Upper Room

- rowing Jesus across the sea

- going into town to get a donkey so He could ride into the city (Jerusalem)

- handling the finances

- feeding the 5,000 (finding the boy with the bread and fish, organizing the people into groups of 50, passing the food, collecting the leftovers...)

The disciples who were with Jesus, **faithful in doing errands, are now released and appointed to teach and preach the Word of God.** Once they had walked and talked and lived with Him. They had been willing to take on the load of the menial duties, doing many of the necessary tasks behind the scenes, so that the Master could spend time with the Father in prayer and then minister to the hurting masses around Him.

Then Jesus left. He returned to the Father. And those who had served Him faithfully in the small things were given greater responsibilities.

The reward for their faithfulness in carrying out those little tasks was being given greater assignments. They had proved themselves. The Father knew they could be trusted to complete the further assignments that would be given to them. And the disciples now find that, in order for them to do what has been entrusted to them, THEY need someone to ASSIST them.

God GIVES the talents. He USES the desires. He TRAINS. He TESTS. He PROVES. Then He ADVANCES.

Being Faithful

Let's keep reading in Acts 6. It gets better and better. For soon we find that those who were selected (the seven men of good report) to assist the disciples were indeed faithful:

❑ They performed their duties.

❑ They sought no glory.

❑ They were there when needed.

We see that because of their faithfulness, God entrusts His servants with greater responsibility.

Look at STEPHEN. **He had made a decision to be available.** To be there to meet the needs of the widows and needy. And God noticed him. Before long, Stephen (Acts 6:8-10) was doing great wonders and miracles among the people. There was such an anointing upon him that even those of the synagogue who were disputing with Stephen could not resist the wisdom and the spirit by which he spoke.

This incident proves that the spiritual power promised to the apostles was NOT LIMITED to them, but was for ALL BELIEVERS. God had noticed Stephen's purity of heart — his attitude — and his faithfulness in the small things. And He had moved him into opportunities which brought manifestations of the power and anointing of God working through him.

PHILIP was also one of the seven. **He had made himself available.** He "waited upon the tables." I imagine he had responsibilities including collecting food, clothing, money for the needy. He probably organized people and duties and heard lots of complaints and disputes among the people. There were lots of widows in those days, lots of beggars, lots of people on the streets. It was not a glorious job that Philip had.

But Philip chose to be there. He made a decision to be faithful. He determined to serve with a joyful heart, and he shared his love of the Saviour on a daily basis to all those hurting people around him.

The Bible doesn't specify how long Philip served unnoticed. But we see him in Acts 8 being used mightily of God to preach the Word with great power in Samaria. There were so many miracles and deliverances among the people that the whole city was filled with joy! (Acts 8:5-8).

A little later on, we see Philip being used to convert the Ethiopian eunuch, who in all likelihood was able to bring about a great revival when he returned to his own country.

By the time of Acts 21:8, Philip is called "Philip the evangelist." But, he is known not just as the evangelist . . . No, his faithfulness in those early days of "waiting on tables" is recorded in the same phrase as a part of his description: *"Philip the evangelist, WHICH WAS ONE OF THE SEVEN."*

". . . one of the seven." Think about it.

CHAPTER 3

The Noblest Calling

During the last ten years, I have seen, heard, and talked to many people — especially Bible students — who are called into the ministry. Many know the Word, and there is a definite anointing upon their life. But they keep

"waiting upon their ministry . . .

and waiting upon their ministry . . .

and waiting upon their ministry."

Many think that God is going to drop them into a dynamic preaching, teaching, healing ministry standing before thousands of people.

I've seen some wait so long that they are now backslidden. Others are working in secular jobs, although they have been called out of those jobs. They are trusting in their employers and not in God.

Some of their marriages have fallen apart. Their families have split. Many have financial problems. And practically all have lost their joy.

Why?

There are several reasons. The main one is —
the enemy is a master of lies and deception.

Since the birth of the early church — and the
POWER and GROWTH it experienced **due to the
willingness of the lay people to serve** — the
devil has made it his business to STOP that power
and growth **by perverting the very concept of
servanthood.** Yes, he has tried to hinder
FINANCES to stop the Church . . . but his massive
effort has been to stop the HUMAN resources. The
manpower. The cooperative effort. The unity of purpose. He has set out to cover up and to squelch the
talents and abilities . . . and the anointing upon the
LAY PEOPLE.

To accomplish his deception, one lie the enemy
has used is to demean the word "servant." Servant
is the word Jesus used to describe Himself. It is the
word the apostle Paul used when proclaiming that
he was a "love slave" — that is, a slave for life, by
choice, to the Lord Jesus and to the Gospel. Yet, the
word "servant" has for centuries had a different
slant cast upon it.

In this nation, which has been chosen by God to
send forth the Gospel into all the world, "SER-
VANTHOOD" (which, as shown in Chapter 2, is one
of the keys to sending that Gospel forth) has come to
mean — people captured and enslaved by their masters; people working to no end and with no reward;
Africans working on the plantations; immigrants in
the fields; people of a lower class; the uneducated

who have no formal training and who wait upon the socially elite and wealthy.

So has the mind thus been deceived.

Because we have been trained in this erroneous thinking, many good people who want to help in God's work do not. Because THEIR HEAD has stopped the serving that THEIR HEART wants to give.

How We Perish

The WORK OF THE MINISTRY — such a wonderful work to be involved in! So many have missed the blessing of being involved in God's work by falling into the deception of believing that serving is degrading.

Yet there are those who have not been deluded in respect to servanthood, and who have willing hearts, only to fall into another trap. The enemy has dissuaded many good men and women of God from getting involved in the work of the ministry by telling them they are not QUALIFIED. Not capable. Not trained. Not anointed. Lies! Lies! Lies!

So, God's Secret Agent, a beautiful Christian full of love and power, refrains from going to the hospital to pray for people because he is afraid he may say the wrong thing.

A gifted elderly woman spends lonely days and hours in her home because she feels she is not qualified to do anything which can be of value in the church office.

Graduates from a Bible School hop from church to church, trying to learn more and more before they feel anointed enough to start their own study group.

Thus the "work of the ministry" is left to the "professionals" — the clergy — those who have gone to seminary or other institutions of higher learning, or whom God has specially ordained to preach, teach and minister to the sick.

Oh, how we perish for a lack of knowledge.

An Early Grave

Not too long ago I was invited to speak to a church conference to which many pastors of a particular denomination had been invited. The pastor who had invited me had a church of around one hundred people.

The day before the visiting pastors arrived for the conference, the host pastor mowed the grass around the building and trimmed the hedge.

The next day, he got to church several hours prior to any people arriving so that he could:

- ❏ unchain the parking lot
- ❏ open the doors
- ❏ turn on the air-conditioner and lights
- ❏ dust off the pews
- ❏ set up the platform
- ❏ arrange the sound equipment

❑ test the microphones

❑ fix the flowers

❑ unlock doors to nursery and supplies

❑ plus numerous other things pertaining to the service.

When the people began to arrive, he stood at the door and shook their hands and handed them a bulletin he had typed and xeroxed himself.

The service began, and our host pastor

❑ opened with announcements

❑ welcomed the visitors

❑ led praise and worship with his wife playing the piano

❑ received the offering

❑ sang a special song during the offering

❑ and then preached his message.

When he had finished preaching, he

❑ prayed for the sick

❑ dismissed the people

❑ ran to the back door to shake their hands

❑ after the building was empty, he made sure all the air-conditioning and lights were turned off

❑ locked the doors

❑ chained the parking lot off

❏ took several of the visiting pastors out to eat

❏ went home to collapse before returning for the evening session.

I was grieved in my spirit. This pastor had SO MANY who could help him, but who in ignorant bliss sat comfortably in their pews and watched the services "just happen" — while their young and energetic "professional" pastor was literally digging himself an early grave.

"Their Place" — "My Place"

Earlier in the year, I had a similar experience with another pastor. Except this was perhaps even more tragic. I had been contacted and invited to come and speak to the congregation on "getting involved in the work of the ministry."

A few weeks after the invitation was given, the pastor called and cancelled the books he had ordered to give out to his people, and told me it might be best for me not to come. He said, "You see, our people don't understand that THEY are to do the work. In fact, if you come, I will lose my church. I was told BY MY ELDERS AND BOARD that they were not there to do any work.

"They have been taught that they are not allowed to go into the hospitals, prisons, or nursing homes . . . THEIR place is to work and make money and pay their tithes into the church. And MY place as the pastor is to do the work of the ministry and care for the church, both the building and its people."

What a tragedy. His people are being robbed of blessing, purpose, and fulfillment because of a lack of knowledge.

Breaking Free

Another pastor and his wife whom we have known for many years told my wife and me a similar story. He had a wedding to perform one day. They arrived at the church early and did all the things necessary to get the building ready. He busied himself both indoors and outdoors while his wife decorated the church, set up candles, arranged flowers, got items ready for communion, etc.

After the wedding, our pastor friend got ready to sign the marriage certificate and his hand was shaking so badly he couldn't sign it. That is when his wife said, "That's it. We're giving up this church."

This couple is still in ministry today, though not behind a formal pulpit. They are doing more ministry out of their home than many pastors of church congregations and are a tremendous blessing to the body of upcoming ministers.

But, because of the lack of HELPS in operation, plus his wife having enough sense to realize that if he continued doing all he was doing she would no longer have a husband in good health . . . they both made a decision that God would get more glory from ministers who served Him WISELY even if from a home base, than He would from two highly anointed, broken down, exhausted, burned out pastors with no help.

It appears that the master of deception has worked a work in the Body of Christ. **IT'S TIME TO BREAK FREE** and be about the Father's business! Get it down into your spirit now and forever that:

❏ SERVING IS THE NOBLEST OF CALLINGS. Jesus, the Son of God, now seated at the right hand of the Father, proclaimed that He came to be a servant.

❏ YOU DO HAVE TALENTS, SKILLS AND ABILITIES THAT GOD NEEDS, YOUR CHURCH NEEDS, AND THE HURTING MASSES AROUND YOU NEED.

❏ YOU ARE UNIQUE. YOU ARE A VITAL PART OF THE BODY OF CHRIST.

❏ GOD HAS A SPECIALLY ORDAINED FUNCTION FOR YOU.

❏ THE WORK OF THE MINISTRY IS FOR ALL BELIEVERS. Not just the "professional" in the pulpit. The job of the apostle, prophet, evangelist, pastor and teacher is to *"PERFECT THE SAINTS FOR THE WORK OF THE MINISTRY"* (Ephesians 4:12).

Then the Lord said to Moses, "Summon before me seventy of the leaders of Israel; bring them to the Tabernacle, to stand there with you. I will come down and talk with you there and I will take of the Spirit which is on you and will put it upon them also; they shall bear the burden of the people along with you, so that you will not have the task alone."

Numbers 11:16,17 TLB

The Living Bible, Paraphrased. ©1971 by Tyndale House Publishers, Wheaton, Illinois.

CHAPTER 4

The Duplication Principle

In the Old Testament, following the great exodus of God's people from Egypt, Moses had his hands full. He had approximately 3 1/2 million people to look after. It seemed they were always complaining, quarreling among themselves, and continually coming to him for counsel.

Moses began to get tired. Frustrated. Weary. In fact, the burden of all the people became so great upon Moses that God saw his plight was too much for him. He sent Moses' father-in-law, Jethro, by for a special visit ...

EXODUS 18:13,17-25

And it came to pass on the morrow, that Moses sat to judge the people: and the people stood by Moses from the morning unto the evening ...
And Moses' father in law said unto him, The thing that thou doest is not good.
Thou wilt surely WEAR AWAY, BOTH THOU, AND THIS PEOPLE that is with thee: for this thing is too heavy for thee;

THOU ART NOT ABLE TO PERFORM IT THYSELF ALONE.

Hearken now unto my voice, I will give thee counsel, and God shall be with thee: Be thou for the people to Godward, that thou mayest bring the causes unto God:

And thou shalt teach them ordinances and laws, and shalt shew them the way wherein they must walk, and the work that they must do.

Moreover thou shalt provide out of all the people ABLE MEN, such as fear God, men of truth, hating covetousness; and place such over them, to be rulers of thousands, and rulers of hundreds, rulers of fifties, and rulers of tens:

And let them judge the people at all seasons: and it shall be, that every great matter they shall bring unto thee, but every small matter they shall judge: so shall it be easier for thyself, AND THEY SHALL BEAR THE BURDEN WITH THEE.

If thou shalt do this thing, and God command thee so, THEN THOU SHALT BE ABLE TO ENDURE, and all this people shall also go to their place in peace.

So Moses hearkened to the voice of his father in law, and did all that he had said. And MOSES CHOSE ABLE MEN out of all Israel, and made them heads over the people, rulers of thousands, rulers of hundreds, rulers of fifties, and rulers of tens.

God spoke of Moses as being the "meekest of all men" (Numbers 12:3). Meekness in that context had the meaning of being humble, seeking to do the will of God with a pure heart, being gentle, compassionate, obedient. Apparently, Moses had such a pure, undemanding heart that he attempted to do all things for all men past the point of human capabilities.

So God had to intervene. He sent Jethro even as He would have sent a prophet to instruct Moses. And, basically, Jethro told Moses that if he didn't start delegating some responsibilities, he was going to kill himself.

Fortunately, Moses thought that was a pretty good idea and was obedient to God's plan.

However, a little later on the multitude of people again began to be too great a burden for Moses. This time Moses went to the Lord with his frustrations, and said in a nutshell, "Lord, You've got to do something about this or kill me!" (Numbers 11:14,15).

The Lord's instructions brought relief to Moses and joy to the camp:

NUMBERS 11:16,17,24,25

> *And the Lord said unto Moses,* **Gather unto me seventy men** *of the elders of Israel, whom thou knowest to be the elders of the people, and officers over them; and bring them unto the tabernacle of the congregation,* **that they may stand there with thee.**
> *And I will come down and talk with thee there: and* **I will take of the spirit**

> **which is upon thee, and put it upon
> them;** *and they shall bear the burden of
> the people with thee,* **that thou bear it
> not thyself alone.**
> *And Moses went out, and told the people
> the words of the Lord, and gathered the
> seventy men of the elders of the people, and
> set them round about the tabernacle.*
> *And the Lord came down in a cloud, and
> spake unto him, and took of the spirit that
> was upon him, and gave it unto the sev-
> enty elders: and it came to pass, that, when
> the spirit rested upon them, they prophe-
> sied, and did not cease.*

There was an interesting reaction when the seventy (who were now anointed by God with the spirit
that was upon Moses) began to prophesy. Joshua —
who was Moses' servant from youth, and who later
led the people into the promised land — got upset
and said (Numbers 11:28), *"My lord Moses, forbid
them!"*

But to Joshua's surprise, Moses replied, *". . .
Enviest thou for my sake? Would God that all the
Lord's people were prophets, and that the Lord
would put his spirit upon them!"* (Numbers 11:29).

You see, **Moses saw that if he had workers
and helpers:**

❏ THEY could pray for the people;

❏ THEY could counsel the people;

❏ THEY could take some of the load off of him;

❏ And HE, as leader, could spend time in prayer, seeking God's face for direction.

No wonder Moses wished that *"ALL THE LORD'S PEOPLE WERE PROPHETS, AND THAT THE LORD WOULD PUT HIS SPIRIT UPON THEM!"* He could be a much better LEADER by having PEOPLE help him to carry out the great work God had called him to do.

Note, my brethren, that in this day of the Church, the desire and the wisdom of Moses has been fulfilled. What he saw as a small sample of what God could do has become a reality in potential. For the SPIRIT that God then put UPON the people to help and assist in the work of the ministry, He has now placed WITHIN the people. Every believer now IS ABLE to PROPHESY, to PRAY for the people, to MINISTER to the needs, to ASSIST the pastor in whatever capacity there is need, to fulfill the great work God has for US to do.

God's Plan For Your Talents

If this is true — and God's Word is true — why don't "men of God" teach their people the importance of serving?

There may be several reasons.

There are pastors — yes, pastors — who, unfortunately, operate in fear. Fear that if they train their people to do the work, then one day someone in the congregation is going to be able to do a better job. And then he, the pastor, will lose his church to one of his trainees.

The fallacy is, if a pastor is smart enough and wise enough to train his people because of a genuine desire to increase the kingdom and to minister to the hurting people, he will only experience multiplication — never decrease. God multiplies seed sown. Whether it be finances, gifts, talents, abilities or wisdom. I have never known of any pastor who trained and equipped and taught his people to get involved in the work of the ministry who experienced anything other than DEEPER COMMITMENT from those in his congregation, plus tremendous CHURCH GROWTH. It is a spiritual law.

Another reason is, there are some men of God who get so wrapped up in the vision God has given them that they don't take time to tell or train someone else how to accomplish it. Or, when they do tell someone else, the people they are trying to teach do not hear, or do not follow instructions. Then, when something does not get done the way the man of God wanted it done, he feels that he should have just done it himself.

You see, when God calls a man and places him in that office, he is anointed of God. And if the man of God sees a job not being done, or not being done according to his standards, because of the burden and passion of his vision, he will go ahead and do the job himself.

If he is not careful, the man of God will get so involved and bogged down in doing the work of the ministry that he will either not have the time to — or he will not have the energy to — study, pray, and hear God. The result will be that HE will not be spiritually prepared to stand before the people to teach and train THEM, and eventually:

❑ The Word will stop or become dry.

❑ Signs and wonders will not be happening.

❑ The masses will not be there (or be brought into the Kingdom).

Moses suffered (mentally, emotionally and physically) because of his willingness to do everything for all of the people. God had to rescue him. God gave Moses a plan and showed him how to work the plan.

In the age of the Church, God even betters the plan:

❑ He sets ministry gifts in the Church to teach and train the people.

❑ He places the people each one in His own special position and function in the Body.

❑ He fills every believer with His Spirit.

❑ He endues them with His power.

❑ He then directs them to GO and to USE THEIR TALENTS — FOR THE WORK OF THE MINISTRY.

CHAPTER 5

You are Part of God's Plan

God's Word has set forth an assignment for the Church in Ephesians 4:11-16. We have made reference to this Scripture previously, but let's take a good look at it again.

EPHESIANS 4:11-16

And he gave some, apostles; and some, prophets; and some, evangelists; and some, pastors and teachers;
FOR THE PERFECTING OF THE SAINTS, FOR THE WORK OF THE MINISTRY, for the edifying of the body of Christ:
Till we all come in the unity of the faith, and of the knowledge of the Son of God, unto a perfect man, unto the measure of the stature of the fulness of Christ:
That we henceforth be no more children, tossed to and fro, and carried about with every wind of doctrine ...
But speaking the truth in love, may grow up into him in all things, which is the head, even Christ: From whom the whole

body fitly joined together and compacted by that which EVERY JOINT SUP-PLIETH, ACCORDING TO THE EFFECTUAL WORKING IN THE MEASURE OF EVERY PART, maketh increase of the body unto the edifying of itself in love.

Verse 12 indicates that the job of those set in ministry offices of leadership is to **"perfect the saints"** for the work of the ministry. "Perfecting the saints" can also be translated "training" them or "equipping" them for a job that God has cut out for them.

Who Are The Saints?

The Saints are BELIEVERS. Saints are those who have chosen Christ Jesus as Lord and who believe that God's Word is true.

If you are a pastor/teacher/evangelist/prophet/apostle — you should be getting the believers ready to go out boldly and well equipped with spiritual knowledge and power TO DO THE WORK OF THE MINISTRY.

If you are a believer — you should be getting under the teaching of those who will set you in the right direction, train you and equip you. **YOU should be DOING the work of the ministry wherever the Spirit of God directs you.**

What is The "Work of The Ministry"?

It is simply being about the Father's business.

Whatever is needful to be done to evangelize the world is the Father's business.

The Body is made up of believers fitly joined together. "Every joint supplieth" or "every believer supplieth" means that **there is something for each and every member of the Body of Christ to do.** Everyone can pray. Everyone can lay hands on the sick. Everyone can lead people to Christ. But then there are **special** talents and abilities and skills which God places in every individual. Besides praying and witnessing and getting people saved, healed, or set free from oppression — which we ALL are directed to do in Mark 16 — we each have a special ability which God needs for us to use so that the whole Body can function efficiently.

Why Isn't Everyone Involved?

If the believer has not been trained to do the work of the minister — the pastor does it all, or tries to do it all, himself. As a result, we have this tremendous separation between the ministers of the Body of Christ and the believers or laity.

Many believers want to help. They want to get involved. However, they feel that since they are not called to a pulpit ministry, or they are not in a teaching ministry or holding crusades or revivals, they are to sit back and watch the pastor.

Yes, there is a season when we should sit under the Word and wait upon our ministry. (By the way, "wait" in the Greek means "to serve" — not to sit around doing nothing!) A new convert may need a little time to get his life together, and just get built up in his spirit as he begins to understand and function as a "new man."

But, so often, we as ministers put so many restrictions on our new converts that it is almost impossible for them to get plugged in and involved. The church will set twelve weeks of training at this, six weeks of training at that, and eight weeks of training at this . . . until the energy, drive, enthusiasm and excitement which first fills the believer begins to regress.

As the young believer sits under the Word, he learns that he is a man under authority: so, since he doesn't want to create a hassle, he will just sit and be a good boy (or girl) and feed on the Word. He listens to his peers and to the ministers and depends upon what they say. And he begins to form his opinions from what man says instead of reading and studying God's Word for himself and hearing what God is telling him.

Unfortunately, most Christians do not realize they have a ministry, because most pastors do not fully understand Ephesians Chapter 4. This is why it is so vitally important to be a pastor who teaches and equips your people to get involved in the work of the ministry . . . and to be a believer who hunts out a church where you can get involved.

Do not perish for a lack of knowledge.

Pastors, do not stifle your church growth by allowing your people to sit comfortably in their pews.

People, do not hinder the blessings, the sense of purpose and the fulfillment that comes when you realize that **YOU are an important part of the purpose and plan of God in the earth. He needs you to do your part to accomplish that plan!**

A Miracle is Squelched

In 1977, I went to Tulsa, Oklahoma, for a tremendous meeting of God. I was a new believer, six months old in the Lord, and was full of expectancy.

During that meeting, God had me in the right place at the right time every night. I saw a number of very evident healings and miracles.

On the final evening, Saturday night at 10:15 p.m., the speaker laid hands on me, and I began to hear out of my right ear — in which I had been deaf since the age of two.

I was so excited about the healing that I went back to my hometown and shared it with those wonderful people who had taken me under their wing. When they heard of the marvelous thing that God had done, I was told that God doesn't heal today. Some asked, "Are you sure?" "How do you know you can hear?" Others whom I thought would get excited commented skeptically, "That's nice."

I had come back to my hometown with hearing restored in my right ear. But I was questioned with so much doubt and unbelief by so many individuals that I actually lost my healing. In fact, I had been told I was lying — with the reason being stated that,

"If God still heals today, why are there so many sick in the church, and why isn't the entire deaf section in this fellowship healed?"

So I became confused. Faith left. And the hearing in the ear left. Then I left. Left the fellowship and those precious people who loved God so much, but who had cast doubt upon His goodness and power and willingness to heal.

The reason I share this is that there are many new Christians coming into the Kingdom every day. And many in leadership capacities fail to teach the whole truth of God's Word. Just as some do not teach the healing power of God, others do not teach the directive in the Word that every believer should be active and involved and using his talents in doing the work of the ministry.

Your Part

God wants you — every pastor, every leader, every man, woman or child who is a believer — to be a part of the greatest revival the Church has ever known. You are important! You are vital!

The pastors can't do it all. The evangelists can't do it all. God has placed every believer in the Body just as He desires. He has a plan for you and has already given you the gifts, talents and skills which He can use if you will let Him. You are called. You are ordained.

Some may say, "But I thought only those professional men and women of God were ordained for ministry." ORDAINED means "separated, called, anointed," or better yet, "identified to do a **specific job**." According to Ephesians 4:16, YOU are ordained for ministry.

There is need of YOU in the Body of Christ. Not just to sit and get fed on the Word. But to get active and be a working, functioning member of the Body.

When I became a Christian, I wanted to get involved and help. I wanted to DO SOMETHING FOR GOD. I was so on fire that I wanted to tell everyone about my new life. But, who was I? At that time, I did not know my authority. I didn't know who I was in Christ. I shared my testimony at church and with individuals, but, basically, I was taught and expected to sit and feed on the Word. So I purposed to get fed . . . going from meeting to meeting, town to town, church to church.

I was running all over the country to hear my favorite preachers, getting fatter and fatter spiritually, because I was told to sit and feed on the Word.

For a while, since I was young in the Lord and my zeal and enthusiasm outran my knowledge, this was perhaps good advice. However, NO ONE EVER TOLD ME WHEN I WAS READY TO GET INVOLVED. I learned a lot about God's love. And through branching out to sit under high caliber ministers, I learned who I was in Christ, and about my authority, and about many of God's wonderful gifts and promises to me. But, as full as I was getting, no one ever told me when or how to start giving it out. I knew what God could do for me — but I didn't know what I could be doing for Him.

*But God has arranged all the parts in the
one body, as He wished them to be —
each one of them according to His own
plan.*

I Corinthians 12:18

Combined translations from:
The New Testament in Modern English by J.B. Philips, ©1960, Geoffrey Bles, Lta.
The New Testament: An American Translation by Edgar J. Goodspeed, ©1923, Univ. of Chicago
The New Testament: A New Translation by Olaf M. Norlie, ©1961, Zondervan.

CHAPTER 6

You are an Extension of the Arms of Jesus

During the last several decades, there has been much talk about a revival coming. Teachers have taught it. Pastors have preached it. Evangelists have encouraged it. Prophets have prophesied it. It has been said that the greatest revival the Church has ever known is yet to come.

Are we ready?

*   *   *

We have laid forth the groundwork in Chapters 1 through 5, which, if put into practice, can pave the way for this great revival.

How? By realizing that there is no way the pastors/teachers/evangelists/prophets/apostles can do the job alone. The Bible indicates that WE are responsible for spreading the Gospel throughout the world. When the world is evangelized, Jesus can return! We have need of every single believer in the Body of Christ to get active in whatever role or capacity he is able.

First Corinthians 12:27-29 explains that there are many callings in the Body of Christ, that not everyone has the SAME calling, but that everyone has A calling. The same chapter, verses 20-22, tells us how important each member is to the functioning of the whole body. We simply can't get the job done in the earth without every member doing his or her part! It's a glorious assignment! And God has already given you the talents and abilities you need and which He needs.

Let's zero in for a while on the setting forth of the ministry of HELPS. Have you ever wondered what the Ministry of Helps is? It's HELPING!

Chapter 1 gave a beautiful illustration of the Ministry of Helps in the secular world. Remember ... the beautiful, spotless span of beach that looked as if it were always that way naturally? But in looking behind the scenes, we saw that the loveliness didn't "just happen." There was concentrated effort on the part of faithful workers who worked day in and day out unnoticed.

Many people think that a church service "just happens." Or an evangelistic crusade ... or a miracle service or a Campmeeting "just happens."

We described three pastors in three situations where the lay people had never been instructed, or encouraged, or motivated to get involved — and how these pastors were frustrated, exhausted, nearly burned out.

Where there is motivation and instruction, a desire will be birthed in the people. Enthusiasm will grow. Because they will see that GOD set forth HELPS as a MINISTRY. Right along with prophets, apostles, teachers, evangelists and pastors.

One must not only understand the need for a ministry of helps, but recognize that Helps is a vital part of God's plan. Helps is a ministry. The people who are working behind the scenes are GOD'S SECRET AGENTS!

For the benefit of those who are getting excited about serving God, let's look a little deeper at the Ministry of Helps!

Understanding The Ministry of Helps

The ministry of helps is listed by Paul with the other ministry gifts in 1 Corinthians 12:28 — *"And God hath set some in the church, first apostles, secondarily prophets, thirdly teachers, after that miracles, then gifts of healings, HELPS, governments, diversities of tongues."*

People called to the ministry of helps have basically the same burden and vision for sharing the Good News of the Lord Jesus Christ as the minister or speaker.

They include a great variety of people behind the scenes — maintenance personnel, sound men, secretaries, administrative personnel, counselors, bookkeepers, greeters, ushers, nursery workers, hospital visitation workers, Bible Fellowship leaders, advisory board members, and others. **Virtually every member of the church congregation has something to offer.**

The ministry of helps will play a vital role in these last days, because as churches grow, and as other meetings become larger, it will be impossible for one person — the pastor or man of God in charge — to make all of the arrangements.

It's sad to say, but many pastors today, as we saw in Chapter 3, are still responsible for everything from preaching to mowing the grass to bookkeeping. The pastor needs to be freed of all these duties so he can spend time in prayer and in the Word, preparing for his main duty — ministering the Word of God to the people.

If the pastor is free to function in this capacity, without becoming bogged down with the other technical cares of the church's function, he will be a beautiful channel through whom the Holy Spirit can do HIS work in this last hour.

For this to happen, the pastor needs men and women serving in the area of "helps" who will:

❑ flow with the supernatural anointing of God,

❑ be sensitive to the Spirit of God,

❑ all speak the same thing,

❏ be in unity and love toward one another,

❏ and toward the Body of Christ as well.

The first step in insuring that the above happens is for the pastor and congregation to recognize that THE MINISTRY OF HELPS IS A MINISTRY.

For example, in too many cases, people still look upon church ushers merely as "bucket passers." But when you have a group of ushers working as a team, properly trained and developed, the person ministering up front can be assured of three things:

❏ There will be order in the service.

❏ The Holy Spirit will have freedom in the service to perfect His work.

❏ There will be reverence toward the work of the Holy Spirit.

When these things are assured, the Body of Christ will be able to move into new realms of ministry, where the gifts of the Spirit and the supernatural power of God will flow as never before.

Disciples in The Helps Ministry

The disciples were involved in the helps ministry as they accompanied Jesus in His ministry.

LUKE 8:1

And it came to pass afterward, that he [Jesus] went throughout every city and

*village, preaching and shewing the glad
tidings of the kingdom of God: and **the
twelve were with him.***

The disciples served in whatever capacity was
needed. They instantly obeyed in doing what Jesus
asked them to do. We get a clearer picture of this in
the Scriptural account of the feeding of the five
thousand. Jesus had been teaching the people all
day and knew they were tired and hungry. Moved
with compassion, He directed the disciples to minister to their need:

MARK 6:37-43

*He answered and said unto them, Give ye
them to eat. And they say unto him, Shall
we go and buy two hundred pennyworth of
bread, and give them to eat?
He saith unto them, How many loaves
have ye? go and see. And when they knew,
they say, Five, and two fishes.
And he commanded them to make all sit
down by companies upon the green grass.
And they sat down in ranks, by hundreds,
and by fifties.
And when he had taken the five loaves and
the two fishes, he looked up to heaven, and
blessed, and brake the loaves, and gave
them to his disciples to set before them;
and the two fishes divided he among them
all.
And they did all eat, and were filled.
And they took up twelve baskets full of the
fragments, and of the fishes.*

The disciples were a vital part of the feeding of the five thousand (and these were just the men — think of all the women and children there must have been!). Jesus needed some help; and the twelve functioned in the HELPS ministry:

❑ ORGANIZING the masses of people,

❑ GUIDING them where to sit,

❑ DISTRIBUTING the food as Jesus directed,

❑ PICKING UP the leftovers.

Again, the disciples served in the ministry of helps as they assisted Jesus in the healing of blind Bartimaeus.

MARK 10:46-49

> *And they came to Jericho: and as he went out of Jericho with his disciples and a great number of people, blind Bartimaeus, the son of Timaeus, sat by the highway side begging.*
> *And when he heard that it was Jesus of Nazareth, he began to cry out, and say, Jesus, thou son of David, have mercy on me.*
> *And many charged him that he should hold his peace: but he cried the more a great deal, Thou son of David, have mercy on me.*
> *And Jesus stood still, and commanded him to be called. AND THEY CALL THE BLIND MAN, SAYING UNTO HIM, BE OF GOOD COMFORT, RISE; HE CALL-ETH THEE.*

In this instance, there was a throng of people around Jesus. He heard the cry of Bartimaeus and **directed the disciples to get him and bring him safely** through the crowd to Him. As they fetched the blind man, **they also encouraged him, ministering faith and peace to him.**

You can see in each of these Scriptural accounts that the **disciples were an extension of the arms of Jesus.** In other settings, they went into town to get the donkey's colt for Jesus for His triumphant entry into Jerusalem. And they did all of the tasks involved in preparing the Upper Room for the last supper Jesus would share with them.

If Jesus needed the assistance and help of the disciples, isn't it quite feasible that pastors and other ministry leaders today need to follow His example?

God's Agents In Action

Early this year, the pastor of my church revealed to the congregation that we would be taking steps to be obedient to further instructions he had received about winning the lost to Christ. The vision had been with him for some time. It was now time to act.

Pastor announced that beginning in January, he would be holding monthly evangelistic tent crusades in low income housing projects across the city.

It was my privilege (on a volunteer basis) to

search out information on tents and have the responsibility of purchasing the initial tent. Along with the purchase of the materials came the responsibility of learning how to use them and train others.

Our congregation has been trained to be soulwinners. They have also been equipped as believers to be aggressive in the work of the ministry. People caught hold of Pastor's vision and ran with it.

At this writing, we have held six crusades. The number of people whose lives are changed has increased continually. Because of not only a pastor who is faithful and obedient to God's vision, but also believers who have gotten caught up in that vision, the Word is being taken to the harvest field where signs and wonders follow.

At the last crusade, over one hundred adults and children were added to the Kingdom of God. At the crusade prior to that, the four leading drug dealers in the complex ALL were saved. Healings have occurred which enabled people to stay in their own home instead of going to that of a relative or a nursing facility.

Why? How? Because of one man's vision and faithfulness to God? In part, yes. But could he have done it alone?

At the present time, not counting all of those who are on the staff at our church or who already had been volunteering on a regular basis, scores of individuals from all walks of life have worked to put these crusades together. Here are some of the duties which have been enthusiastically performed:

- ❑ **Door knockers** — bus loads of lay people who for weeks prior to each crusade canvass the territory, inviting people to the crusade, telling them about Jesus, winning some to the Lord before the event ever occurs.

- ❑ **Truck drivers** — to load and unload and transport all of the equipment to the site of the crusade.

- ❑ **Tent raisers** — men who are faithful every Friday and Saturday that there is a crusade to put up and tear down the tent, heaters, chairs, tables, etc.

- ❑ **People to transport and run sound equipment.**

- ❑ **Assistants to work with the children's ministry** — monitors and counselors who minister Jesus' love to the hundred or more deprived children who attend each crusade.

- ❑ **Food collectors and preparers** — to be in charge of providing a snack lunch on Saturday for those who attend the crusade, PLUS prepare tables, food, beverages for Sunday dinner for those who are bussed to the church.

- ❑ **Bus drivers** — a new bus is added to the bus ministry each month. Drivers and assistants or monitors are needed for each bus.

❑ **Ushers** — to assist the pastor in the adult ministry and to assist the children's ministry in the tent.

❑ **Overseers of the clothing ministry** — to collect, sort and distribute clothing to the needy.

❑ **Medical team** — professional physicians donate their time to set up a clinic and see individuals at the housing projects who have physical needs. Assisting them are not only volunteer nurses, but lay people who talk with the people, organize them, pray with them, and write down information for the physicians' records.

❑ **Counselors** — lay people full of the Word of God minister to the new converts concerning salvation, baptism of the Holy Spirit, and their various physical or spiritual needs.

❑ **Telephone workers** — to follow through and minister God's love to those who have accepted Christ.

Isn't this a beautiful, living illustration of the BELIEVERS BEING INVOLVED IN THE WORK OF THE MINISTRY! Isn't it profoundly obvious how multitudes of lives can be affected by the working together of many members of the Body — rather than leaving it all to one "professional" pastor?

Your Assignment

Jesus HELD FAST TO THE SPECIFIC THINGS TO WHICH HE WAS CALLED, having the disciples perform many duties that simply complemented and strengthened what He did. He was constantly about the Father's business.

Men of God today must also be totally free to do one thing — to be about the Father's business! When this becomes so, with the ministry of helps performing its duties in an excellent manner, the Body of Christ will step into a new realm of ministry. The gifts of the Spirit will operate fluently; healings will occur en masse; the Word will go forth with power, authority and might; and we will begin to experience this great end-time revival!

Believers must keep the man of God free from becoming bogged down with the cares of the ministry. We cannot allow the nitty-gritty details and constantly having to run everything to bind up the time and energy of the one who should be wholly dedicated to seeking God and ministering His Word. For when the man of God is hindered, the work of the Holy Spirit is hindered. Neither the man with the vision nor the God who gave it to him is able to fulfill what has been assigned him.

Whether you realize it or not, YOU HAVE BEEN GIVEN A COMMISSION TO BECOME AN EXTENSION OF THE ARMS OF JESUS as you assist His chosen ones in their respective ministries. Often, we speculate, "Oh, it must have been wonderful to work alongside of Jesus. What an honor to prepare the Passover for Him or to go to town and get a donkey for Him to ride."

But, my friend, right now, in this time and place, you have the honor of not only working alongside of Him . . . but you have the opportunity to have a significant role in bringing Him back as KING OF KINGS AND LORD OF LORDS!

CHAPTER 7

Goals for Growth

God has chosen each one of us and has given us all certain abilities, skills and talents to be used for the building of His Kingdom. As we seek Him, we will discover our place in the Body and exactly how we can assist in the great task that the Church has before it.

As we are enlightened by the Word of God and see that we are each to be involved in ministry, the desire and enthusiasm to serve will ignite! There will be no holding back!

We must now — as with any job or assignment — find out what personal qualifications are necessary. What does the Master expect from the ones who represent Him? There are definitely qualities necessary to successful performance in the secular world. Likewise, there are Biblical principles which we must have operating in our lives in order to be successfully used in God's work.

*   *   *

In Chapter 2, we discussed briefly the choosing of the seven who would take over the duties of daily ministrations to the widows. Ministering to the needs of the poor and widowed was most assuredly a responsibility of the Church. However, the twelve disciples, who had now been called into preaching and teaching and traveling ministries, were getting bogged down with these duties. They did not have time to spend in the presence of the Lord and prepare for their ministry of the Word. They needed some people functioning in the ministry of helps!

How would they choose their assistants? What standards should be set for involvement in God's work?

In Acts 6:3, we are given some of the qualities that were required for the seven men who were to be selected to help the disciples. *"Wherefore, brethren, look ye out among you seven men of honest report, full of the Holy Ghost and wisdom, whom we may appoint over this business."*

The qualities for assisting in the work of the ministry were set forth as:

1. Being of a GOOD REPUTATION or OF AN HONEST REPORT (men of integrity).

2. Being FULL OF THE HOLY GHOST. (They were all filled with the Holy Spirit.)

3. Being FULL OF WISDOM. (Both **practical wisdom** to run the business aspect of their ministry and the **wisdom of God** to minister the Word of God.)

As we examine the Scriptures, other qualities are revealed which those who desire to represent Jesus must develop. Set these qualities as "GOALS FOR GROWTH" for your life.

You Must Have a Single Eye

To walk with a single eye is to walk with your body, soul and spirit filled to overflowing with the life of God. You can overflow with the life of God as you fill your mind with the Word of God, meditate upon His Word, and maintain a goal of DESIRING TO PLEASE THE HEAVENLY FATHER WITH ALL THAT YOU SAY AND DO EVERY MINUTE OF THE DAY.

MATTHEW 6:22

> *The light of the body is the eye: if therefore thine eye be single, thy whole body shall be full of light.*

You Must Work As Unto The Lord

Your work as a volunteer — an able minister — God's Secret Agent — must be "as unto the Lord." If you are working to please the man of God only, or working to please other people more than pleasing the Father, you will never find satisfaction in what you do.

COLOSSIANS 3:17,23

> *And whatsoever ye do in word or deed, do all in the name of the Lord Jesus, giving*

*thanks to God and the Father by him. And
whatsoever ye do, do it heartily, as to the
Lord, and not unto men.*

You Must Be Filled With The Word of God

In the following verses, you will see that the
Word of God is your "life" and your "health." You
cannot develop to a point of excellence in serving in
the work of the ministry without God's life and
God's health working in you and through you. They
are yours if you simply take time daily to "feed on
the Word of God."

PROVERBS 4:20-22

*My son, attend to my words; incline thine
ear unto my sayings.
Let them not depart from thine eyes; keep
them in the midst of thine heart.
For they are life unto those that find them,
and health to all their flesh.*

You Must Be Strong in Faith

How do you become strong in faith?

ROMANS 10:17

*So then faith cometh by hearing, and
hearing by the word of God.*

Faith comes as you spend time studying and
meditating upon the Word of God, allowing the
Word to take root in your spirit — not just in your

head! Take time daily in the Word and in fellowship with the Father to develop your life of faith. The Word also says that "... *The just shall live by faith*" (Romans 1:17b).

As you grow in faith, you will learn to call those things forth that be not as though they were. You will trust in the ability of the Holy Spirit to direct you, and you will have success in your endeavors to serve in whatever capacity He leads.

You Must Be Led By The Spirit of God

You will develop sensitivity to the leading of the Holy Spirit as you spend time with the Father. Spend time in the Word. Spend time in prayer. Spend time in quietness before Him.

ROMANS 8:14

> *For as many as are led by the Spirit of God, they are the sons of God.*

You Must Speak Faith-Filled Words

What you say turns the events of your personal life around, and it also has a direct effect on the quality of excellence with which you serve in the work of the ministry. Be a person of words that are faith-filled, positive, edifying and loving — for you receive what you SAY.

MARK 11:23

> *For verily I say unto you, That whosoever shall SAY unto this mountain, Be thou*

removed, and be thou cast into the sea; and shall not doubt in his heart, but shall believe that those things which he SAITH shall come to pass; he shall have whatsoever he SAITH.

You Must Control Your Tongue

As you assist in the work of the ministry, whether you are leading people to Christ, praying for the sick, helping as a volunteer worker in the church — in whatever capacity God has called you — the words that come forth from your mouth will have a vital bearing on your effectiveness.

You will have opportunities to build up people's faith, help them receive their healing, lift up the brokenhearted, encourage a fellow worker. You can actually govern situations and attitudes around you with the power in your tongue. Use it wisely.

On the other hand, when you are working closely with individuals, you will be exposed to various opinions and even some criticisms about this or that — be they geared toward other people or the way things are run. Be careful to let no negative words come out of your mouth, but only words which are edifying, encouraging and which bring peace.

JAMES 1:26

If any man among you seem to be religious, and bridleth not his tongue, but deceiveth his own heart, this man's religion is vain.

EPHESIANS 4:29-32

Let no corrupt communication proceed out of your mouth, but that which is good to the use of edifying, that it may minister grace unto the hearers.
And grieve not the holy Spirit of God . . .
Let all bitterness, and wrath, and anger, and clamour, and evil speaking, be put away from you, with all malice:
And be ye kind one to another, tender-hearted, forgiving one another, even as God for Christ's sake hath forgiven you.

You Must Be Filled With The Compassion of Jesus

Over and over in the ministry of Jesus, the Word of God says that "He was moved with compassion." That must also be your motive — to touch others with the compassion of Jesus that they might be set free.

Your compassion will develop as you spend time learning about Jesus, and determining to walk in His steps. Spend time in His presence, and His compassion will begin to flow through you, enabling you to feel what others feel and hurt when others hurt, for one purpose — to set the captives free!

You Must Walk In Obedience

No matter what your age, you will never outgrow the need to walk in total obedience; first, obedience to God, and then obedience to those in authority over you.

JEREMIAH 7:23

But this thing commanded I them, saying, Obey my voice, and I will be your God, and ye shall be my people: and walk ye in all the ways that I have commanded you, that it may be well unto you.

ISAIAH 1:19

If ye be willing and obedient, ye shall eat the good of the land.

Your first obligation is always to God. Secondly, you must walk in obedience to the authority placed over you. With these priorities correct, you will have a vital part in maintaining unity and harmony in the ministry in which you serve. Have a willingness to show honor and respect to the pastor and/or to anyone he has placed in a position of authority over you.

HEBREWS 13:17

Obey them that have the rule over you, and submit yourselves: for they watch for your souls, as they that must give account, that they may do it with joy, and not with grief: for that is unprofitable for you.

Being obedient to God, and to the one(s) He has placed in authority over you sets the pace and atmosphere for working in excellence as God's Secret Agents.

You Must Walk In The Power of God

You need to walk daily in the power of God with which He has equipped you. You may have many opportunities to yield to discouragement, deceptions, or temptations from the enemy . . . But ". . . *greater is he that is in you than he that is in the world"* (1 John 4:4).

You Must Walk In The Might of God

As you are involved in doing the work of the ministry, you will need an inner reserve of spiritual might. This prayer from the Scriptures is powerful and will have a great effect in building you up as you pray this way daily:

EPHESIANS 3:14-19

> *For this cause I bow my knees unto the Father of our Lord Jesus Christ,*
> *Of whom the whole family in heaven and earth is named,*
> *That he would grant you (insert your name here), according to the riches of his glory, TO BE STRENGTHENED WITH MIGHT BY HIS SPIRIT IN THE INNER MAN;*
> *That Christ may dwell in your (name) hearts by faith; that ye (name), being rooted and grounded in love, may be able to comprehend with all saints what is the breadth, and length, and depth, and*

height;
And to know the love of Christ, which pas-
seth knowledge, that ye (name) might be
filled with all the fulness of God.

You Must Be Faithful

Learn to be faithful in the little things. Your faithfulness and positive attitude as you accomplish the small tasks, the sometimes unpleasant tasks, will be noticed. God trains His children one step at a time; as they prove their faithfulness in the small things, He can promote them to greater responsibilities.

LUKE 16:10

He that is faithful in that which is least is
faithful also in much: and he that is
unjust in the least is unjust in much.

Your faithfulness will also be a tremendous blessing to the minister or ministry which you serve. The fewer cares the man of God has to be concerned with, the more effective he can be in his calling.

PROVERBS 25:13

As the cold of snow in the time of harvest,
so is a faithful messenger to them that
send him: for he refresheth the soul of his
masters.

HOWEVER...

PROVERBS 25:19

*Confidence in an unfaithful man in time
of trouble is like a broken tooth, and a foot
out of joint.*

Strive to be such a blessing to the one you are
representing that you will be like a breath of cool
snow on a hot day — not like a toothache or a broken
foot!

You Must Always Be Dependable

Faithfulness and dependability go hand in
hand. The qualities you develop in your personal
life carry over into your ministry. Be someone that
others can count on. If you say you will do something, keep your word. When you are asked to do
something, follow through with that task to completion! Let it be said about you, "When 'Joe' is in
charge of something, we know it's going to get done
and get done right."

You Must Prefer Others Above Yourself

Jesus said that a truly great man is one who is
willing to be the servant of all. What He was
teaching the disciples was to learn to think of God
first, others second, and then yourself. You will
train yourself to be sensitive to those around you —
their thoughts, their concerns, their needs, their
desires. Show them Christlike love working
through you in all situations.

ROMANS 12:10

Be kindly affectioned one to another with brotherly love; in honour preferring one another.

You Must Be Free of Envy and Strife

Allow no place for envy and strife in your personal life or in your work with the ministry. The Word says that envy is as rottenness of the bones (Proverbs 14:30). Strife will not only upset you to the point that you cannot function, but it will bring distress into the entire group, project, or ministry you are assisting. Don't let the devil even get a toehold into God's work by getting into strife!

JAMES 3:16

For where envying and strife is, there is confusion (tumult, unquietness) and every evil work.

Learn to rejoice over your brother's blessings, honors and special recognitions. As you truly rejoice with your brother, blessings will come your way.

ROMANS 12:15

Rejoice with them that do rejoice, and weep with them that weep.

You Must Walk In Instant Forgiveness

You will have many opportunities to have your feelings get hurt as you are involved in the work of the ministry. You will be working shoulder to shoulder with many types of personalities; some are bound to conflict with yours. Don't let it become a challenge to forgive those who offend you. Rather, let it be a privilege to keep your spirit man so quickened with the Word that you will find it joyous and easy to walk in instant forgiveness toward all men.

MATTHEW 6:14,15

For, if ye forgive men their trespasses, your heavenly Father will also forgive you: But if ye forgive not men their trespasses, neither will your Father forgive your trespasses.

Another passage of Scripture puts it this way:

LUKE 6:37,38

Judge not, and ye shall not be judged: condemn not, and ye shall not be condemned: forgive, and ye shall be forgiven. Give, and it shall be given unto you; good measure, pressed down, and shaken together, and running over, shall men give into your bosom. For with the same measure that ye mete withal it shall be measured to you again.

Many times these verses are limited to "financial" giving in our thinking and application. However, this same kind of giving in other areas will come back to you in like measure, in like kind, as spoken forth in the Word — in giving FORGIVENESS, LOVE, COMPASSION, GENTLENESS,

WISDOM, KNOWLEDGE, UNDERSTANDING, TIME, SKILLS, TALENTS.

You Must Be A Doer of The Word

Your involvement in the work of the ministry necessitates "doing the Word" and not just hearing it. You will have multitudes of opportunities to put the Word of God into action and to put your faith into action. Look forward to the opportunities! It's the most exciting life in the world to watch God perform through you, as you just take the step of action required to allow Him to work.

JAMES 1:22-25

> *But be ye doers of the word, and not hearers only, deceiving your own selves.*
> *For if any be a hearer of the word, and not a doer, he is like unto a man beholding his natural face in a glass:*
> *For he beholdeth himself, and goeth his way, and straightway forgetteth what manner of man he was.*
> *But whoso looketh into the perfect law of liberty, and continueth therein, he being not a forgetful hearer, but a doer of the work, this man shall be blessed in his deed.*

You Must Be An Intercessor

You can break down Satan's barriers in your own life through intercession. Likewise, as you join in with group intercession before every church service, you will be able to break down Satan's work before it has a chance to start. And you will create a spiritual atmosphere which puts every person who comes in a position to receive from God.

In these last days, with the spiritual forces at warfare all around us, intercession is a must for every believer. Time must be spent daily building yourself up so that you will operate with a strong spirit (Jude 20) — whether it be in the home, on the job, or in doing the work of the ministry.

Time must also be spent praying in direct opposition to the enemy's designs against you, your family, your church and its leaders, your nation's leaders, and all whom the Lord would lay upon your heart. We all need to be strengthened daily by corporate concern for one another and fervent prayer for the Body of Christ to be multiplied throughout the earth.

1 TIMOTHY 2:1-4

> *I exhort therefore, that, first of all, supplications, prayers, intercessions, and giving of thanks, be made for all men;*
> *For kings, and for all that are in authority; that we may lead a quiet and peaceable life in all godliness and honesty.*
> *For this is good and acceptable in the sight of God our Saviour;*
> *Who will have all men to be saved, and to come unto the knowledge of the truth.*

As you earnestly strive to develop each of the "goals for growth" mentioned in this Chapter, you will find that the Lord will profoundly work with you, enabling you to reach beyond your human capabilities.

- ❏ You will increasingly be changed and conformed into the image of Christ.

- ❏ You will find that you have more and more opportunities to be involved in the work of the ministry.

- ❏ You will truly be GOD'S SECRET AGENT on assignment!

If you welcome a prophet because he is a man of God, you will be given the same reward a prophet gets. And if you welcome good and godly men because of their godliness, you will be given a reward like theirs.

Matthew 10:41 TLB

CHAPTER 8

Rewards of Serving

Praise the Lord! If you have read this far and have gotten excited about your place in the work of the ministry, you are ready to be enrolled as one of God's special Secret Agents! If you are one of those fortunate ones who has already committed time and energy to serving, I trust that the words of this book have offered some additional enlightenment and enrichment for you. In either case, I guarantee this Chapter to be a blessing.

Expect A Reward

Hebrews 11:6 says, *". . . he that cometh to God must believe that he is, and that he is a rewarder of them that diligently seek him."*

In every instance in the Bible where God commands obedience, He also promises a reward. He says, so to speak, "You do this, and I'll do this."

There are some great rewards in store for those who make a quality decision to open up their heart and seek God's direction in the area of serving. As each member of the Body begins to function as God intended, **you can expect good things to happen. You can expect rewards.**

Examine Your Motives

First, however, let us examine the motivation — the motives — behind the deeds. Why are we getting involved? What do we expect to transpire from our obedience?

The reason we serve is because we love God. We have a desire to find out His will and to be obedient to it. He says there are rewards, there are blessings to the obedient; and He wants us to expect those blessings. Yet, He does not want "receiving" to be our motive.

God promises certain benefits to the tithers, to those who give financially. Yet, He is pleased if our motivation is to increase the Kingdom, to free the captive, to heal the sick. He wants us to plant in faith, and believe for the blessings to come back to us; yet, we are not to have the attitude of "giving IN ORDER to receive."

It is much the same with the decision to be obedient to God in other areas. If we give simply to get, our heart and attitude need to be changed. The wrong motives are present. However, when we give out of a pure heart, joyfully, unselfishly, then as we continually walk in that attitude — yes, we can and should expect God's Word to work on our behalf. We should look for the returns to come — in His way and in His time — and KNOW THAT WE CANNOT OUTGIVE GOD.

I have known students and lay people who have made themselves available for a task with the attitude of, "I'm going to serve in this lowly position for a while so I can become a leader." There have even been some who quoted one of the Scriptures I teach — "If you are faithful in the small things, God will make you ruler over many things" — while telling me their intent in serving was to be promoted, hired by the ministry, or otherwise exalted. God could not advance those persons. He did not. They have never become leaders in any respect.

Let our desire and motivation be: to be conformed into the image of Jesus. Jesus gave himself.

If you are giving your time, your abilities, skills and talents as unto the Lord, you are the kind of servant Jesus exemplified. If you have decided that you are going to be faithful in the little things just because God has enabled you and asked you to do them — and you are willing to keep on doing those little things cheerfully for as long as He wants you to — then you have the kind of attitude that He can develop and prepare for other responsibilities. Do you get the picture?

If your motives are pure and as you are faithful and offer your time and energy as unto the Lord, you can then expect and look for HIS rewards!

Heavenly Rewards

One of the greatest rewards that comes to believers — those who know Jesus as their personal Lord and Saviour — is an eternal home in heaven.

He said, *"In my Father's house are many mansions . . . I go to prepare a place for you"* (John 14:2).

The Bible is clear in declaring that there is a home prepared for us. This home is ours to claim for eternity. It is a place where God will provide for us, forever, in answer to our saying "Yes" to His Son, Jesus Christ.

But there are indications in the Word of God that there is "more."

1 CORINTHIANS 3:11-15

> *For other foundation can no man lay than that is laid, which is Jesus Christ.*
> *Now if any man build upon this foundation gold, silver, precious stones, wood, hay, stubble;*
> *Every man's work shall be made manifest: for the day shall declare it, because it shall be revealed by fire; and the fire shall try every man's work of what sort it is.*
> *If any man's work abide which he hath built thereupon, **he shall receive a reward.***
> *If any man's work shall be burned, he shall suffer loss: but he himself shall be saved; yet so as by fire.*

Nothing will be ignored in eternity! What a tremendous motivation for God's servants! **Nothing goes unnoticed** by the One who really counts. Even the most obscure of God's servants who labors faithfully will be observed by the Heavenly Father; and his **works will be judged by**

the attitude and spirit in which they were performed.

We live in an award-oriented world. In the world system, you perform a certain function and you expect a certain reward. So called "greater" functions are entitled to "greater" rewards.

We need to get our thinking trained according to the Heavenly system. Some of us tend to think a person who ministers to the masses will have far greater rewards than the one who ministers to a few. However, God tends to look at: **Did we DO what we were ABLE to do with the ABILITY He gave us?** (Remember the parable of the talents? Matthew 25:14-29).

God looks at QUALITY. This means He observes motives. He knows the reasons people do what they do. He notes whether they are done in the power of the Spirit or the power of the flesh.

When our works are carried out for motivations of the flesh, they are judged in Heaven to be as "wood, hay, stubble." They will be burned up by fire; nothing will remain, except the saved soul of the individual.

When our works are performed in the power of the Spirit, they are likened to the servant's heart of the Master; and though tried by fire, they shall remain as "gold, silver, precious stones!"

God will determine the QUALITY of every man's work. And when you stand before Him, you can be sure that **He is faithful. He will**

remember how you have ministered to the saints and sought to bring glory to His name in the earth.

HEBREWS 6:10

> *For **God is not unrighteous to forget your work and labour of love,** which ye have shewed toward his name, in that ye have ministered to the saints, and do minister.*

It is marvelous to know that God is always tuned in to what we are doing. So many times I have felt that what I did was so small, so unimportant. Other times I have known very well that what I did was VERY important (why, no one else could have done it!!) and NO ONE NOTICED! But God did! This is why I love those examples Jesus gave: the little widow woman giving the greatest gift of all when she gave her last penny; Mary washing Jesus' feet with her tears and pouring the expensive perfume on Him (Jesus said her deeds would be recorded forever as a testimony of her love); and the poor sinner man who beat his breast knowing that he needed God's mercy (while the Pharisees stood deep in their self-righteousness). Hallelujah! God sees it all. He sees into the heart.

Earthly Rewards

We do live in this earth, though we are not of it. God intended for us to have benefits in this life as well as in our eternal life. Let's look at some of the rewards we can expect as we walk in God's will for our life and are obedient to His calling.

Job's friends were not a great comfort to him in his afflictions, but they did have a knowledge of God's principles:

JOB 36:7,11

> *He withdraweth not his eyes from the righteous...*
> *If they obey and serve him, they shall spend their days in prosperity, and their years in pleasures.*

As we OBEY God and SERVE Him, we can expect to have PLEASURE — **that is, joy and fulfillment in our life** — and PROSPERITY — **freedom from lack.**

Isaiah 1:19 promises that, *"If ye be WILLING and OBEDIENT, ye shall eat THE GOOD OF THE LAND."* There are two requirements here: to be "willing" — that is, to have the right attitude. And to be "obedient" — to follow through to completion of the assignment. THEN you can expect to "eat the good of the land." The GOOD of the land denotes all kinds of earthly rewards — financial needs met, good health, protection and well-being for yourself and your family, joy, peace of mind, fulfillment.

There is another reward which the faithful servant may anticipate... although he is not to make it his goal or priority. Scripture indicates in several reference points that if we are faithful in the small things we are given to do, then God will entrust us with more. The more faithful you prove yourself to be, the more responsibility will be given to you.

MATTHEW 25:21

His lord said unto him, Well done, thou
good and faithful servant: thou hast been
faithful over a few things, I will make thee
ruler over many things . . .

So the reward for your faithfulness is more
responsibility! Just keep in mind that both the
Father and the man of God you serve will be taking
note of your attitude and motives before promoting
you.

Then there are the **intangible rewards** which
will have perhaps the more lasting effect on you and
those around you. Those of you who function properly in your position in the Body, no matter how
obscure that position, are responsible for the
making of a ministry which is "well oiled, running
smoothly, efficient, producing" for the Kingdom of
God.

Your job will link together with the jobs of others
to insure that the OVERALL JOB of the Body of
Christ — the CHURCH — gets done. **You will have
a part in bringing back the King!**

God didn't save you just to take you to Heaven!
He didn't call you into service in order to rob you of
your time. Could you imagine what it would be like
if everyone were praying, giving, and doing their
part in the Kingdom?

Our prayers and our life's motives should be:

"LORD, USE ME.

LET YOUR LOVE FLOW THROUGH ME.

ORDER MY STEPS.

HELP ME TO DO MY PART IN MEETING THE NEEDS OF ALL THE HURTING PEOPLE AROUND US.

THROUGH THE POWER OF YOUR HOLY SPIRIT, I AM WILLING.

THANK YOU, JESUS!"

The Ultimate Reward

Let's look at a very special promise for the faithful servant:

❏ The one who realizes that it is not just the professional man of God who is called to do the work of the ministry,

❏ The one who knows that no act of love is too small for God to notice.

❏ The one who is there when he is needed because he knows God has put him there and he has allowed God to direct his steps.

We get an insight into God's reward system in Matthew 10:40-42:

> *He that receiveth you receiveth me, and he that receiveth me receiveth him that sent me.*
> *He that receiveth a prophet in the name of a prophet shall receive a prophet's reward; and he that receiveth a righteous man in the name of a righteous man shall receive a righteous man's reward.*
> *And whosoever shall give to drink unto one of these little ones a cup of cold water only in the name of a disciple, verily I say unto you, he shall in no wise lose his reward.*

Servants of God, no matter what your placement is in the Body, no matter how small your task, BECAUSE OF YOUR FAITHFUL INVOLVEMENT BEHIND THE SCENES, YOU HAVE AS MUCH A PART IN EVERY CHANGED LIFE THAT WALKS DOWN AISLES AS DOES THE MAN BEHIND THE PULPIT.

You may not be the one bringing the person to the Lord, but through your faithful efforts to do what you are able to do, EVERY PERSON WHO WALKS DOWN THOSE AISLES WILL GREET YOU IN HEAVEN. They may not know you here, but they will know you there!

AND EVERY CROWN OF REWARD THAT IS GIVEN TO THE MAN IN THE FOREFRONT — YOU WHO HAVE SERVED IN THE BACK- GROUND — WILL ALSO RECEIVE. For he who gives a drink of water to a prophet will receive a prophet's reward: He who helps carry the load of the man of God will receive the man of God's reward!

How many crowns do you have? What has been your involvement? It's not too late! The servants who came in at the eleventh hour were paid the same amount as those who had worked all day (Matthew 20:6-9).

Paul in 2 Timothy 4:6-8 is looking back over his life. He tells Timothy to fight a good fight. To complete the course. Finish the assignment. EVERYONE HAS A COURSE TO RUN. GOD WANTS YOU TO GET ON THE TRACK. RUN IT TO WIN. YOU ARE IMPORTANT. HE NEEDS YOU TO FULFILL YOUR PURPOSE, YOUR COMMISSION TO HIS GREAT ARMY.

One day you will stand alongside of Paul. You will be in that same line. Paul ran the course. And he told Timothy a crown awaited him. We think of Jesus — the King of kings — being worthy of a crown . . . but it had been revealed to Paul that he, too, FOR BEING AN EXTENSION OF THE ARMS OF JESUS, HAD A CROWN AWAITING HIM.

2 TIMOTHY 4:7,8

> *I have fought a good fight, I have finished*
> *my course, I have kept the faith:*
> *Henceforth there is laid up for me a crown*
> *of righteousness, which the LORD, THE*
> *RIGHTEOUS JUDGE, SHALL GIVE*
> *ME AT THAT DAY: AND NOT TO ME*
> *ONLY, BUT UNTO ALL THEM ALSO*
> *THAT LOVE HIS APPEARING.*

AND THEN, AS WE GATHER BEFORE THE THRONE ON THAT GREAT DAY . . .

REVELATION 4:9-11 (NAS)

> *And when the living creatures give glory*
> *and honor and thanks to Him who sits on*
> *the throne, to Him who lives forever and*
> *ever,*
> *The twenty-four elders will fall down*
> *before Him who sits on the throne, and*
> *will worship Him who lives forever and*
> *ever, AND WILL CAST THEIR*
> *CROWNS BEFORE THE THRONE,*
> *saying,*
> *'Worthy art Thou, our Lord and our God,*
> *to receive glory and honor and power; for*
> *Thou didst create all things, and because*
> *of Thy will they existed, and were created.'*

WHAT A SCENE! WHAT A GLORIOUS DAY AWAITS US! All of God's servants are before His throne, bowing in worship having cast all crowns before their Lord and King. JOINED TOGETHER WITH ALL THE SOULS THEY HAVE HAD A

PART IN BRINGING TO THAT GLORIOUS MOMENT! HALLELUJAH!

And then, the King of kings and Lord of lords looks out over the vast sea of souls, and says, TO YOU — THE USHER, THE GREETER, THE PARKING LOT ATTENDANT, THE DOOR-KNOCKERS, THE FOOD COLLECTORS, THE BUS DRIVERS, THE NURSERY WORKERS, THE INTERCESSORS, THE NURSING HOME VISITORS, THE MUSICIANS, THE CHOIR MEMBERS —

"I HAVE SEEN YOUR HEART,
MY BROTHER,
MY SISTER.

I HAVE TAKEN NOTE OF
WHAT YOU HAVE
DONE IN MY NAME.

WELL DONE, GOOD AND
FAITHFUL SERVANT.

COME AND ENTER INTO
THE JOY OF YOUR LORD."

CHAPTER 9

You Are God's Agent!

As you have read through the previous chapters, I trust that you have felt an excitement stirring within you! There is no greater place to be than right in the middle of God's perfect will for you! And to REALIZE THAT:

- ❑ You have a gift that He wants you to use for His glory!

- ❑ You are a valuable member of the Body of Christ!

- ❑ You do have something to contribute!

- ❑ God needs you!

God knows right where you are at this moment. Perhaps you have been aware of a need for involvement, and you have had that desire but have been discouraged or told to wait. Your heart is right, your motives are right, but either approval or circumstances have not worked out yet.

Let the words of this book inspire you! Let the Spirit of God guide you! Don't throw in the towel... Keep in mind that the ministry God has given you includes the world outside of the church building:

❑ In the community

❑ In the hospitals

❑ In the nursing homes

❑ In your place of employment

These are the places where you can see the world through the compassionate eyes of Jesus... and the world can see Jesus through you.

Some of you have thought of yourself, "I don't know what I can do." God has given to YOU — to every believer — the ministry of reconciliation.[1] He says, *"I have made you ABLE MINISTERS of the New Testament."*[2] Your calling, your ordination is from God. It is irrevocable.

There is not a thing in the world that you cannot accomplish when you know who you are in Christ, when you know your calling, and when you know you are in God's perfect will.

Get your eyes off of past defeats, failures, frustrations. You are forgiven. You are living in Grace. "It is God working in you who will cause you both

[1]2 Corinthians 5:18
[2]2 Corinthians 3:3-5

TO WILL and TO DO His good pleasure."[3] Your enablement is from Him. When you live for Him and seek His Kingdom first, all that you face or accomplish will be not by your power and your might, but by His Spirit working through you.

If you are willing and take the step of faith to begin to get involved, from this point God will assume the responsibility of removing the hindrances or obstacles in order for you to complete your assigned task.

Just imagine what you can do when you begin to operate in the power of the Holy Spirit and not out of your own strength. See yourself operating in God's wisdom — in God's energy — in God's resources — in God's power.

Don't Miss The Boat

It's time to ask yourself, "What have I ever done for others? What am I doing now? What will I be noted for when I am gone from this earth?

Most of our life is spent living for ourselves. Making an income. Providing for the family. Putting the kids through school. These things are needful. But they do not need to consume you.

Jesus demonstrated by His example — you must be about your Father's business.

National statistics show that 10 percent of the people in all churches do 90 percent of the work. Ten

[3]Philippians 2:13

percent provide most of the church's finances. Let's begin to reverse these statistics.

Throughout the previous chapters, we established the need for God's able ministers and their vital importance to the multiplication of His Kingdom. Are you ready to ask God, "What can I do?" I am convinced that if you seek God and allow Him to direct your desires, He will show you exactly how and where He can use you.

By now you know that if you want God's best and perfect will for your life, you need to move toward it with corresponding actions. Faith is putting words into action. When you believe in something, you move toward it by stepping forward.

Peter let down the net . . . after he had fished all night without a bite. Why? Because he had faith in the Master's words. So, in faith Peter moved toward it with works — or corresponding action. The result was, faith that was supplemented with action triggered his miracle. He caught so many fish the net could not hold them!

You are called to help spread the Gospel. Your church has the same calling. Your pastor has a vision. Get behind him and help him to fulfill the vision God has given him.

If you had lived during the time of Noah and did not help out, you would have missed the boat.

Don't miss the boat!

Put God To The Test

When you are working for the King of kings, your life will be lifted. You will lift those around you. You will be an extension of the arms of Jesus.

The enemy may still tempt you to doubt. He will tell you, "What you do is so small . . . They don't need your help."

But I say to you, "Despise not small beginnings." It may be that you are the one tiny cotter pin that can keep the wheel from falling off. It may be that God wants to use you as a cotter pin. Or it may be that He wants to test your WILLINGNESS in the small things so that He can raise you up into greater responsibilities.

The important thing is, What does GOD want to do in your life? Is He satisfied with the way you have used your talents? Are you satisfied? Or is there something missing in your life?

Ask yourself: "Do I have the courage to find out what God wants?" Will you put Him to the test? I believe you will.

Make A Commitment Today

Look at the card on the last page, and ask God what He would have you do. Find an area in which God can use you. As He shows you the areas you should be involved with, mark them on the card. If an area is not listed, write it down.

We are in spiritual war time. In war time, everyone does something. God is calling His Army to serve.

How wonderful it is to work alongside of Jesus. How thrilling it is to have Jesus working through you:

❑ In hospital visitation.

❑ In preparing food for the needy.

❑ In relieving office workers in the church.

Some may say, "I want to help, but I can't get out of the house. I have no transportation." Do you know you can minister God's friendship and love to others right from the telephone in your own home?

❑ You can call the new converts and talk to them about what their decision means.

❑ You can welcome newcomers to the church.

❑ You can pray for people's needs.

❑ You can invite people to church or to special services.

❑ You can spread the love of Jesus.

If you are ready, say, "YES, LORD! I hear your trumpet! I take a step of faith today, and I will be a part of the End-Time Revival!"

Act now.

Take out the card provided at the end of this chapter.

Fill it in.

Give it or mail it to your pastor.

Or put in the offering bucket.

Let him know he will not have to take on all the work of the ministry, but he can depend upon you to be committed to assist him in the vision!

Make this your confession and prayer as you meditate on the message of this book.

HOLY SPIRIT, LEAD ME INTO ALL THE AREAS WHERE I AM NEEDED.

MAKE ME A DOER OF THE WORK OF THE MINISTRY.

USE THE GIFTS, TALENTS, SKILLS AND ABILITIES YOU HAVE GIVEN ME FOR YOUR GLORY.

DELIVER ME FROM SELFISHNESS.

LET ME BE IN YOUR PERFECT WILL.

RELEASE YOUR ANOINTING UPON ME NOW, THAT I MIGHT FULFILL THE CALLING YOU HAVE GIVEN ME.

IN THE NAME AND IN THE IMAGE OF JESUS, I NOW GO FORTH. AMEN.

...es, I want to become involved and use the skills, abilities, and talents God has given me to assist you in the work He has called you to do. I will stand with you and be committed in the following areas. (MARK THE AREA OR AREAS IN WHICH YOU FEEL YOU CAN BEST USE THE SKILLS, TALENTS AND ABILITIES GOD HAS GIVEN YOU.)

ADMINISTRATION
Accounting
Clerical
Data Entry
Purchasing
Receptionist
Running Errands
Secretarial
Set up Transportation
☐ Airlines
☐ Buses

CHILDREN
Age 0-1/Nursery
Age 2-3/Toddlers
Age 4-5/Pre-School
Age 6-12/Children's Church
Bus Drivers
Bus Ministry Workers
Children's Drama
Counseling
Missionettes
Royal Rangers
Saturday Sunday School
Scouts (leaders/helpers)
Sign Language Class
Special Needs
☐ Mentally Handicapped
☐ Physically Handicapped
Sunday School Teachers

FACILITIES
Carpentry
Cleaning
Construction
Custodial
Electrician
Grounds Care
Lawn Care
Maintenance
Painting
Vehicle Maintenance

MISSIONS
Chaperones
Instructions
Support
Teaching

MUSIC
Band
Choir
Creative Dance (Worship)
Ensembles
Soloists
Worship Leaders

NEW MEMBER/VOLUNTEERS
Phone Calling
Visitation

OUTREACH
Adopt-a-Missionary
Bible Fellowship
(Home groups)
Bus Drivers
Bus Ministry Helpers
Clothing Ministry

☐ Counseling
☐ Benevolent
☐ Bereaved
☐ Chemical Dependency
☐ Drug Prevention
☐ Family
☐ Homosexuals
☐ Marriage
☐ Personal
☐ Suffering
☐ Telephone

☐ Crusades

☐ Evangelism
☐ Neighbor Teams
☐ Personal
☐ Soulwinning

☐ Fellowship of Ministries
☐ Financial Teaching
☐ Food Ministry
☐ Good Samaritan Ministry
☐ Healing Team Ministry
☐ Inner-City Ministry
☐ Jail/Prison Ministry
☐ Jobs Ministry/Placement
☐ Keenagers/Senior
   Citizens (55+)
☐ Legal Services
☐ Men's Ministry
☐ Membership Class
☐ Missions
☐ Monthly Luncheon
☐ New Member Class
☐ Supernatural House Calls
☐ Tape Ministry to Missionaries
☐ This New Life (New Converts)

☐ Visitation
☐ Home/Fellowship
☐ Hospitals
☐ New Members
☐ Nursing Homes
☐ Shut-ins
☐ Telephone Visits

PASTOR/WIFE
☐ Car
☐ Children
☐ Food
☐ House
☐ Yard

PRAYER
☐ Daytime Prayer
☐ Early Morning Prayer
☐ Evening Prayer
☐ Intercessory Prayer
☐ Prayer Chain

PUBLISHING
☐ Advertising Design
☐ Advertising Layout
☐ Artist
☐ Graphics
☐ Media
☐ Proofreader
☐ Public Relations

☐ Publishing
☐ Bulletins
☐ Newsletters
☐ Books

RECREATION
☐ Ballet
☐ Basketball
☐ Bowling
☐ Class Picnics
☐ Coaching
☐ Golf
☐ Gymnastics
☐ Officiating
☐ Softball
☐ Volleyball
☐ Other _____

SCHOOLS
☐ Bible Institute
☐ Christian School
☐ Missions School

SINGLES
☐ Activities
☐ Publications
☐ Sunday School Helps
☐ Workshops

SUNDAY/MID-WEEK SERVICES
☐ Altar Counseling
☐ Assemble Printed
   Materials
☐ Assemble Service
   Materials
☐ Audio Technician
☐ Believer's Class
☐ Bible Teacher
☐ Bookstore
☐ Counting Offering
☐ Communion Assistants
☐ Deaf/Hearing Impaired
☐ Greeters/Hostesses
☐ Information Table
☐ Lighting Technician
☐ Nurses/Doctors
☐ Parking Lot Attendant
☐ Pre-Service Set-up
☐ Share-a-Ride
☐ Service Transportation
☐ Sunday School Teacher
   ☐ Assistant
☐ Tape Duplication
☐ Ushers/Hosts
☐ Video Technician
☐ Visitors Reception
☐ We Care Program

YOUTH
☐ Assistants
☐ Band/Music
☐ Bus Drivers
☐ Drama
☐ Teacher

OTHER

_____

_____

NAME (LAST) (FIRST) (MIDDLE I.)

ADDRESS (CITY) (STATE) (ZIP)

PROFESSIONAL SKILLS:

PHONE: (WORK) (HOME)

Yes, I want to become involved and use the skills, abilities, and talents God has given me to assist you in the work He has called you to do. I will stand with you and be committed in the following areas. (MARK THE AREA OR AREAS IN WHICH YOU FEEL YOU CAN BEST USE THE SKILLS, TALENTS AND ABILITIES GOD HAS GIVEN YOU.)

NAME _____ (LAST) ____ (FIRST) ____ (MIDDLE I.)

ADDRESS ____ (CITY) ____ (STATE) ____

PHONE: ____ (WORK) ____ (HOME)

____ (ZIP)

PROFESSIONAL SKILLS: ____

ADMINISTRATION
☐ Accounting
☐ Clerical
☐ Data Entry
☐ Purchasing
☐ Receptionist
☐ Running Errands
☐ Secretarial
☐ Set up Transportation
  ☐ Airlines
  ☐ Buses

CHILDREN
☐ Age 0-1/Nursery
☐ Age 2-3/Toddlers
☐ Age 4-5/Pre-School
☐ Age 6-12/Children's Church
☐ Bus Drivers
☐ Bus Ministry Workers
☐ Children's Drama
☐ Counseling
☐ Missionettes
☐ Royal Rangers
☐ Saturday Sunday School
☐ Scouts (leaders/helpers)
☐ Sign Language Class
☐ Special Needs
  ☐ Mentally Handicapped
  ☐ Physically Handicapped
☐ Sunday School Teachers

FACILITIES
☐ Carpentry
☐ Cleaning
☐ Construction
☐ Custodial
☐ Electrician
☐ Grounds Care
☐ Lawn Care
☐ Maintenance
☐ Painting
☐ Vehicle Maintenance

MISSIONS
☐ Chaperones
☐ Instructions
☐ Support
☐ Teaching

MUSIC
☐ Band
☐ Choir
☐ Creative Dance (Worship)
☐ Ensembles
☐ Soloists
☐ Worship Leaders

NEW MEMBER/VOLUNTEERS
☐ Phone Calling
☐ Visitation

OUTREACH
☐ Adopt-a-Missionary
☐ Bible Fellowship
  (Home groups)
☐ Bus Drivers
☐ Bus Ministry Helpers
☐ Clothing Ministry

☐ Counseling
  ☐ Benevolent
  ☐ Bereaved
  ☐ Chemical Dependency
  ☐ Drug Prevention
  ☐ Family
  ☐ Homosexuals
  ☐ Marriage
  ☐ Personal
  ☐ Suffering
  ☐ Telephone

☐ Crusades

☐ Evangelism
  ☐ Neighbor Teams
  ☐ Personal
  ☐ Soulwinning

☐ Fellowship of Ministries
☐ Financial Teaching
☐ Food Ministry
☐ Good Samaritan Ministry
☐ Healing Team Ministry
☐ Inner-City Ministry
☐ Jail/Prison Ministry
☐ Jobs Ministry/Placement
☐ Keenagers/Senior
  Citizens (55+)
☐ Legal Services
☐ Men's Ministry
☐ Membership Class
☐ Missions
☐ Monthly Luncheon
☐ New Member Class
☐ Supernatural House Calls
☐ Tape Ministry to Missionaries
☐ This New Life (New Converts)

☐ Visitation
  ☐ Home/Fellowship
  ☐ Hospitals
  ☐ New Members
  ☐ Nursing Homes
  ☐ Shut-ins
  ☐ Telephone Visits

PASTOR/WIFE
☐ Car
☐ Children
☐ Food
☐ House
☐ Yard

PRAYER
☐ Daytime Prayer
☐ Early Morning Prayer
☐ Evening Prayer
☐ Intercessory Prayer
☐ Prayer Chain

PUBLISHING
☐ Advertising Design
☐ Advertising Layout
☐ Artist
☐ Graphics
☐ Media
☐ Proofreader
☐ Public Relations

☐ Publishing
  ☐ Bulletins
  ☐ Newsletters
  ☐ Books

RECREATION
☐ Ballet
☐ Basketball
☐ Bowling
☐ Class Picnics
☐ Coaching
☐ Golf
☐ Gymnastics
☐ Officiating
☐ Softball
☐ Volleyball
☐ Other _____

SCHOOLS
☐ Bible Institute
☐ Christian School
☐ Missions School

SINGLES
☐ Activities
☐ Publications
☐ Sunday School Helps
☐ Workshops

SUNDAY/MID-WEEK SERVICES
☐ Altar Counseling
☐ Assemble Printed
  Materials
☐ Assemble Service
  Materials
☐ Audio Technician
☐ Believer's Class
☐ Bible Teacher
☐ Bookstore
☐ Counting Offering
☐ Communion Assistants
☐ Deaf/Hearing Impaired
☐ Greeters/Hostesses
☐ Information Table
☐ Lighting Technician
☐ Nurses/Doctors
☐ Parking Lot Attendant
☐ Pre-Service Set-up
☐ Share-a-Ride
☐ Service Transportation
☐ Sunday School Teacher
  ☐ Assistant
☐ Tape Duplication
☐ Ushers/Hosts
☐ Video Technician
☐ Visitors Reception
☐ We Care Program

YOUTH
☐ Assistants
☐ Band/Music
☐ Bus Drivers
☐ Drama
☐ Teacher

OTHER
_____
_____